AF413212

SPIRIT

Helle Gade

Title: Spirit
Author: Helle Gade
Copyright © 2022 Butterdragons® Publishing
All Rights Reserved

Published by Butterdragons® Publishing
https://butterdragons.com

ISBN: 9789493229778 (ebook)
ISBN: 9789493229785 (hardback)
ISBN: 9789493287280 (trade hardback)
ISBN: 9789493229792 (audio book)

Cover Design by: Dazed Designs

Audio book narrated by Martha Webb

To my darling Lucy Dream Dancer

For Helle, with love

She is a shield maiden of old,
Her gentle nature is her shield
Her heart – steady and vast – is her armour
And her words are like a sword,
Piercing, sharp, and beautiful.
She is a warrior-poet, walking barefoot through waves,
Joined – forever – by her beloved, four-legged
confidant.
Together they stride,
Their bond transcending this world and the next.

by BDP Authors

Spirit

Unconditional Love

She loved me when I was happy
She loved me when I was mad
She loved me when I was sad
She just loved me

My Life

I saw through the sands
The valleys of my life
Ups and downs
Radiant joys
And trembling fears

I see the line I walked
As if I navigated
Through a minefield
Choices spread out before me
A candyland of traps and treasures

Have I made the right choices?
Perhaps, I will know that on my deathbed
Or maybe there is no right or wrong
Only a life to be lived
And lessons to be learned

Fog

Scattered
Thoughts
Drifting
Into
The fog
Chased by
A hungry
Mind

Child's Spirit

She danced through the flowers
Her spirit pure and innocent
A picture of undiluted joy

You might think this a fairytale
A deceitful tale
Told with rose-coloured glasses

Yet this is every child on a meadow
When they are let loose
Without restraint

We adults have only forgotten
How to chase away
The cloud of responsibility

To let loose our inner child
And let love flow unrestrained
As our spirits fly free

Sin

I am not a sin that
You can contain within

I am out there
For all to see

A painful reminder
Of things best forgotten

Wild Wind

He gravitates towards me
I playfully avoid him

He growls loudly
I let out a peal of laughter

No one has ever caught me

His hand snatches my wrist
Burning my skin

I twist, trying to escape
But he pulls me in

Shifting his hands to my waist
I push against his chest

Though, he does not budge
His long hair curtains our faces

He whispers above my lips
Caught you

Tremors run through my body
Through my soul

I was not meant to be caught
A wild spirit I was

He lets out a masculine laugh
Pulling me tight against his slender frame

My soul screams to be free
Fear weakens my being

He steals a kiss, steals my breath
I feel myself melt in his arms

Only one is able to tame the wind
The ruler of mischief and mayhem

I look into his eyes
Seeking the answer

I, the wildest of nature
Have been conquered

I, the wildest of nature
Have been tamed

The Cell

I am sitting in a cell
Of my own construction

Bars cover the windows
Locks bolt the door

I have created this prison
Brick by painful brick

I thought I could make
A safe space to rest

Instead, I unconsciously
Created a prison

With dab grey walls
And anxiety-inducing silence

Thor

The taste of lightning
Is rolling on my tongue
Sweet and spicy
As mead

Its energy
Pouring through me
Igniting every cell
In my body

As the hammer strikes
The thunder follows
Shaking the ground
Beneath my feet

Unleashing
The pent-up energy
Stored within me
In a rush of joy

Little Lies

Little white lies have vicious claws
Even those I tell myself

They amass over time
Drawing tiny rivulets of blood

Which collect into a river
Of misery and pain
Caught in the ecstasy of crisis

Reboot

The fog is heavy today
It surrounds my head
Thick as cotton

Taking away
Memory
Logic
Senses

Locking me
In an alternate universe
Where I am barely sentient

I wonder
If this is what it feels like
To lose my mind

It can last a day
A week
Or a month

Snapping out of it
Seeing clearly again
Is like breaking the surface
Of a vast grey ocean
Taking a deep breath of air

A metaphorical rebirth
All systems starting up
My brain waking anew

Death and the Maiden

His mahogany voice
Full of whisky
Whispered promises
Of nebulous deeds
Star-shattered feelings
In the obscure part
Of my opaque spirit

Revelry ruptures my placid heart
Benevolence flees my body
In search of pleasurable pain
To alleviate the empty space
Left in my dying imagination

Oh, how sweet the memory
Of sublime creation
My Milky Way of artistry
Leaves me with tears of starlight
Filling the river Styx

On my deathbed
His whispers
Destroy and rebuild me
Fortifying my eternal devotion
To his purpose
To his very essence
The other half of my soul

Sinner

I am the sinner
You are the saint
Follow the trace of pain
Deep into the bowels
Of the polluted soul
Feel the excruciating pain
That has spread like poison
Infecting the conscious stream
With agony on the cellular level

Agonizing Waves

A wave crashing over me
My mind crumbles
Under the unfathomable pressure
Pain like no other
Stabbing me repeatedly
Breathing hard
Working through the agony

Ahhhhhh….
The relief is intoxicating
I feel light as a feather
Enjoying the precious feeling
For the short time it lasts
Before the next wave
Crashes over me

Calm

The view calms me
Slow moving clouds
Shrouding the peaks occasionally
The bird of prey screams in the distance
The smell of herbs and flowers in the air

All is peaceful
There is no rush, no stress
No demands
I can let my shield down
Be utterly vulnerable

The ancient mountains
They speak to my soul
And I recognise their voices
Flowing through my being

They speak of the wind
Of the snow and ice
Of the old times
And the birth of the new times

Silence is filling me
Cell by cell, liquifying me
Until I'm nothing more
Than the mist shrouding the peaks

Child of the Abyss

Demons in the flames
Licking my heart
With fiery tongues
Demanding my surrender
Craving my darkness
Claiming that I belong
That the embers of my soul
Were born in the abyss
Bred to be the one
To bring the pain into the light

Agony and madness
Will follow in my wake
As I teach the world
About the outcasts
Sick and disabled
That are being scorned
By all the ignorant people
Cruising through their lives
Blaming the castaways
For their petty problems

Let me teach you
Misery and suffering
With the flames of Hell
I will demolish
Your preconceived notions
Of how the perfect world is
Showing you the beauty
Of physical and mental imperfections
Teaching you
Compassion and understanding

A Little

I am
A little south of sanity
A little north of insanity
A little west of love
A little east of hate

It is all so complicated
Yet so simple
That it should be obvious
But seldom is

I stand outside
The centre of the storm
Looking in
Yearning for the perfect calm

Tension Headache

I feel fragile
The tension
In my neck
Radiating into my skull

I feel like
I could break apart
If I move too fast
Or don't move at all

I feel like crying
Nauseous
And foggy
Tender
And breakable

I feel the pills
As they slide
Down my throat
Hoping for relief
But fearing they won't work

I Am

You can take me
You can break me

But if you, for one second, think
That I will stay broken
You are sorely mistaken

I will pick up every single piece
And reassemble myself

I will be stronger and wiser
I will stand against
The oncoming storm

My Flame
My essence
Were a roaring fire
Though now reduced
To a single flame

I keep them alive
By feeding them fantasies
Taking me out of my body
And into brilliant worlds

Though rooted in place
Curing my wanderlust
Between the pages
I keep them alive

My Princess

The hardest time
Is when I go to bed

The routine of treats
Placement on the Princess' pillow

Are things that hit me hard

Rolling over in my bed
Remembering to be careful

But there is no one to look out for

Waking up in the morning
Not getting sleepy snuggles

Both, my bed and heart are empty

Rain

Raindrops on the window
Running down in rivulets
Tears of the heavens
In their purest form
Cleansing the world
Washing away the dirt
The sorrow and pain
Bringing new life
And freshness to the air
That makes it breathable again

Night Terrors

Tossing and turning
Drenching the covers in sweat
The mind is on a journey
To the deepest, darkest corners
Of your poor soul
Dredging up the foulest fears
That you never knew you harboured
Displaying them mercilessly
In an endless stream of horrors
Terrorising you savagely
Until you finally wake
Shaking violently
Trying desperately to banish
The hellish visions
That cling to your mind
With a demonic strength
Beyond this world

The Reaper

Do not fear death
Living is what can
Make you or break you

The reaper is merely a guide
Towards peace?
The next adventure?
Perhaps nothing...

He is there to great you
With gentle hands
Embrace you with strong arms

He will guide you towards the light
Comforting your soul
As it leaves this life behind

Praise him and be thankful
For he is truly worthy
Of his never-ending purpose
Of bringing peace to weary souls

Poisonous Whispers

My spirit is bloody
A testament
To the horror
That encases me
In a hateful cloud
Of poisonous whispers

In a frenzied rush
I try to purge the toxin
That burns my thoughts
To glue together
The brittle edges
Of my darkened soul

Covetous

It blooms in my ribcage
This feeling
Of spring and wildflowers
Light as a cloud
Warm as sunlight

I want to keep it
To hoard it like a dragon
For the times
When the abyss
Threatens with darkness

Pagan Faith

Walking through the mist
A sense of the ancient Gods
Cocooning me
Boosting my confidence
Encouraging me to move forward
Towards my dreams
Swathed in colours
Shining through the grey
Surrounding my being

I increase my speed
My bare feet dancing
Through the dew-covered grass
As I hear the gentle sound of music
Colourful shadows approach me
On wings heavy with the moisture
From the pine scented air

Tiny creatures emerge from the mist
Carried by silky butterfly wings
By a strong transparent dragonfly
And delicate moth wings
Fluttering around me
Making my heart skip with delight
As I twirl around in the clearing mist
Their song is intoxicating

So, I raise my voice
Joining the ethereal choir
Praising the beauty of the forest
The silver rays of the moon
Breaking through last vestiges of the mist
Enlightening the surroundings
Revealing my dreams come true

He stands at the edge of the clearing
Leaning on an ancient oak
Looking deceptively relaxed
From his long mahogany hair
Antlers adorn his head
His only clothing
A pair of buckskin pants
His luminous eyes
Dark blue as a summer sky
Follow my every move
Increasing my heart rate

A silent noise from behind me
Reveals a stunning woman
Ash blond hair reaching her bare feet
Her body barely covered in a dress
Made by moonlight and stardust
Adorning her head is a reef of mistletoe

I fall to my knees with a bowed head
As the vision of my Lady overwhelms me
Tears of joy and reverence stain my cheeks
As I reach my hands towards her
In a silent prayer of love
Asking for the blessing

I feel her touch through my skin and bones
All the way to my inner-most being
The power of the moon cleansing me
The power of the stars igniting me
My future falling away
Only the present matters
As I pledge my heart and soul
To the Goddess of the Moon

A touch on my shoulder
By the horned God
Tethers me to the ground
Letting me feel Mother Earth below me
Reminding me not to fly away
My mission on Earth is not yet finished
My time of learning has just begun

Revenge

I can hear the blood
Course through your veins
I can smell the sweet flavour
Of what is to come
Revenge!
I take back my pride
With a blade and claw
In a river of blood
I shall celebrate your demise
By sending your soul
To burn in Hellfire forever

Silhouettes

Dark silhouettes
Swaying ominously
Fear creeping over the skin
The heart pounding furiously
Sweat tickling down the back
Startling me into motion

The feeling of being followed
Is suffocating me
Sounds appear louder
And frighteningly close

As I stumble along
I start to hum
Moving purposely towards the lights
Because I will be safe there
Lights are always safe
Or so I thought

Mental Chaos

Riptides
Push and pull
My thoughts
Like a full moon
High and low
Constant movement
Never still

Midnight Gamble

Midnight Chimera
Fabolous or frightening
Never knowing what to expect

I lie down to sleep
Anticipation and apprehension
Warring with each other

I drift towards dreamland
Neurons fire to life
Showing me my dreams come true
Or fears spread out before me

The Crow

He sits on his branch
Watching me intently
With his black eyes
Burning into my soul
Night after night

He is the carrion crow
Awaiting my death
He comes to me
Carried by the silent storm
Telling a tale of agony

I watch him with resigned calm
Neither his look, nor my actions
Will lead to an early demise
The tapestry of my life
Was woven long before my birth

So come, come watch
The herald of my death
Hear him crow
For a taste of my, soon to be
Death

Undying Love

Take my hand
Let me lead you down this path
Let me show you how my soul
Sparkles like the stars
That glitter in the sky
A night-time wonder
Night sky full of diamonds
As the uncut one
Holds your hand

REM

The night is my playground
It is where I let my imagination
Roam free of boundaries
Exploring everything

From the sweetest Nirvana
To the cimmerian shade

From gruelling phantasms
To the highest delights

Oh, the stories I could tell
If only I did not forget them
As soon as dawn arrives
And I, yet again
Join the world of reality

Fractured

I carry my fractured heart
Beneath my broken wing

Blood seeping trough
The snow-white feathers

Dotting the ground
In a pattern of betrayal

My travels have yet to find a cure
So, I keep walking

One day, it will be mended
And my wings will take me to the sky again

Brittle

Cloudy dreams
And hidden fears
A tentative touch
To my brittle spirit
For the world, I will bleed
For you, I will live

Lost Time

War is in my blood
Adrenaline
Coursing through my veins
At the thought of battle

I am a warrior of old
Fighting with honour
Blades dripping crimson
Satisfying my blood lust

I am a being out of time
Misplaced in this
Deceptively peaceful
World of politicians

Truth and battle
Have given way
To honeyed words
And dishonest actions

Wasteland

I rode the wave
Until the sand
Was all I could see

A desert below
A star-filled sky above

I thirsted for more
But touched
Only tiny grains

Lost in an empty
Barren wasteland

The Wild Hunt

Black hounds baying
Witches and gods
Creatures of the night
Running

The game is afoot
Under a lush moon
Pregnant
With the promise of magic

Trough the star light
They run
Trough the veil of shadows
They hunt

Anxiety

A hiss in the shadows
Alarm bells ringing
Dread pooling in my belly
Ice sliding over my skin
Making me tremble in fear

I am being hunted
By an unknown foe

Or maybe not so unknown...
Maybe I just pretend not to remember
Thinking that if I forget
Then it will go away

But it never does
It returns whenever I'm vulnerable
Beating on my senses
Unrelenting and unforgiving

Gloom

She dances in lonely places
Amongst spectres of past mistakes
Surrounded by regret and guilt
Chipping her spirit piece by piece
Until only her shadow is left

Peace

Leaning against the warm rock
The sun is caressing my face
Like mother's gentle touch
Breathing slowly
Inhaling the scent of flowers
Grounding myself
Letting all the worries flow away
Soaking up the heat into my soul
The peace of my surroundings
Renewing my energy
Preparing myself
To face the world again

My Furbaby

The loss of you
Caused a seismic shift
In my entire world

After being together
Every hour of every day for a decade
Your absence hurts so much

You were my pride and joy
My partner in crime
A constant source of cuddles

You left behind a void
A proverbial black hole
Absorbing the joy from my life

The Oncoming Storm

I am the storm
Roaring towards the land
Pushing the waves
Against the shore
Battering the land
Eating away the coast

I am nature
I am wild and fierce

Fear me
And my destructive powers
Let the beasts below
Rejoice in being free
Of human interference
Let them ride my strength

They are my children
They are wild and fierce

Watery Tomb

In the dim light
Of the oncoming night
I hear the cry of a seagull
As my nose fills
With the smell of brine
The waves crash
Against the ancient pier

Tiny droplets
Start to fall from the sky
The tears of the Gods
Mix with my own salty ones
The darkness
And cold of the night
Penetrate my old bones
Making my body shudder
Till I lose my grip of the railings

I hug myself
And send out my prayer
Of gratitude over a long
Well-lived life
I take one step forward
Letting the waves swallow me up
Hoping to see Neptune
Before I'm out of breath

Cold Sky

Midnight sun
A fierce illusion
Stabbing my heart
Hope seeping out
Of the thin cracks
Dissolving into the air
Colouring the sky red

Treasure

I finally found it
A tiny, tiny speck
Of wonderful calm
As if the exposure
Of my soul
Has dimmed a bit
Sure, it brings out new things
Into the sharp light
New fights to be fought
And enemies conquered
But I feel it!
Right at the edge
Of my consciousness
A silent blissful breeze
A treasure!

Freedom

Freedom is an illusion
Your mind is a cage
Your thoughts its inhabitants

We start out as free spirits
Slowly filling the cage
As we grow older

We are told what to do, who to be
And by the time we realise the mistake
It is almost impossible to break free

Sometimes it is easier
To blame the cage
Than keep trying to escape the chains
Of adulthood and society

Narrow Paths

Hands fumbling along the walls
As I travel down the darkened halls
That my mind consists of
Searching for something

Possibly light?
The meaning of life?
Sweet memories?
Me?

White Lilies

He brings me white lilies
And gentle kisses

We dance on nebulas
Full of possibilities

We inhale the clouds
That dreams are made of

As we twirl on a nimbus
Of sparkling fairy dust

In tune with the birds singing
A melancholy song of longing

I am the maiden
He is the reaper

Our love is effortless
Our love is timeless

Roaring

Midnight light
Midnight solitude
Flying on raven wings
Trough the bells of the storm

Crimson poppies
Bleeding in the dirt
Next to my ravished heart
The remnants
Pulsing with magic light

Silver notes
Carry me high in the sky
As I try to reclaim my soul
From those who stripped it from me
And tore my humanity to bits

My Weathered Feelings

She left me on a day
When the sunset
Was a spectacular array of colours
And a rainbow appeared in the north

The days I waited
To retrieve her from the crematorium
The sky was grey and rainy
My mind, much the same

When I got her ashes
The sky was clear and sunny
A storm raging around us
Reflecting my feelings

Now she is home
The wind is silent and birds chirping
The winter sun shines brightly
I am finally at peace

The Veil

The world is no longer the same to me
Things are lurking in the shadows
That never should be seen by human eyes
Things that haunt me in my dreams
Making me jump at every little sound
Cry out whenever I see something
Out of the corners of my eyes
The veil has fallen
And now I'd give anything to un-see it all

Books

They told me to dream
They whispered
Bright fairytales

Of the stars
The centre of the earth
Of worlds beyond fantasy

Of star whales
And men in blue boxes

Of a fellowship
And a ring of power

Of talking animals
And Kings and Queens

Of dragons
And those who ride them

They took me traveling
Through one fantastical world
To the next
In untold hours

Fanning the flame of my imagination
Driving me to continue further
For me to contribute
To share my tales

Star

Oh, darling
I am but a lonely star
On the velvet night sky
Crying glittering tears
That fall to earth
I keep lunacy away
From those
Who prowl the night
Ravenous for sleep
Infusing glorious fables
In their addled brains
Only a pen or voice away
From composing fairytales
That will dazzle the world

Angel

I am the rose angel
Carrying jasmine flowers
At my overflowing bosom
Come to shower you
In white petals of death
To kiss you
With poisonous lips
Sending you towards
The nether worlds
To be embraced
By fire of the lost ones
Burning in eternity
For the heinous sins
That called me from the sky

Lucy Dream Dancer

Life moves forward
But I fucking hate that

It should be curled up
In a ball like me

It should be crying and raging
Against the devastating loss

One minute, feeling dead inside
The next minute, feeling too much

I knew it would happen
Yet it still came as a shock

My insides are screaming in agony
And I don't understand how to…

She took a piece
Of my heart with her

She took the part
That loves unconditionally

The part that she nurtured
Like a delicate flower blooming

They are now one in the veil beyond
And I feel the loss acutely

Prayer

I hear them coming
Fire, walk with me
As I greet my faith
Burn the path behind me
Light up the path before me
Give me strength
When my insecurities
Threaten to overcome me
Enlighten me
When my ignorance
Threatens to overwhelm me
Be my guide
Through this mortal world
As I find my way towards Bifrost

Sisterhood

Rising moon
Above my bowed head
Sisterhood love
Flows in the hands I hold
Mother Earth
Grounding our souls
To the beat of her heart

We are the past
The present
The future

Maiden
Mother
Crone

Censorship

There was a time
Before we had to school our words
A time of reckless fun
That no one was insulted by

Now it seems that people are just waiting
For the opportunity to explode
To take their shit out on others
While playing wounded saints
What has become of the saying
Treat others like you want to be treated?
Where is the compassion?

Friends getting stalked
By crazy strangers
Artist's work being reported
But telling a teenage girl to kill herself
That is okay?

A nipple in a painting is worse
Than seeing a friendly pet being shot
Is that what we are teaching our children?
Nudity is terribly wrong even in art
But violence against the helpless is acceptable?

I cry for the youth nowadays
It is no wonder it has become a me-me-me world

Where is the freedom of speech?
Without being hunted like an animal

Higher powers sit on the throne
Deciding what is right and wrong
Controlling our voices
Controlling our future

Succubus

She took my spirit
Filled it with fire
And left me to burn
Alone in the dark
Cold and despondent
A husk of a man

Limbo

The moment between waking and sleeping
Where everything is possible
Dream and reality mix
And blur the lines of the mind

The shadows conceal you in the early dawn
Night becomes day and day becomes night

A time where your sleeping mind
And waking consciousness
Battle for your attention
Creating phantom pictures

Come Fall

My tears
Fresh
As morning dew
Decorating
The delicate petals
Shining as
Diamonds
Mourning the loss
Of summer
Yet celebrating
The new season
With blood red
Passion

Release

A chasm opening in my chest
Spilling out the darkness
That I have carried for years
It flows before me
Like an ominous cloud
A biohazard for all to avoid
Pain, grief, hunger
Are only a few of the feelings
That are now released
From my battered body and soul
Relief so strong that it shakes my being
Coats me like a new skin
A fragile protective barrier
That brings hope of a lighter life

My Darling

My darling Lucy
I love you so much
I already miss you
Desperately

My little Princess
My heart and soul
I will always carry a piece
Of your heart and soul

My beautiful girl
You were a Mother
Of beautiful pups
A delightful legacy
My crazy Diva

You ruled over the Nullerboys
With a firm paw and yips
The boys will never be the same
And neither will I
I love you!

Acknowledgements

I want to thank Kim Stapf, Ira Myriam and Ben Ditmars for always being there when I need inspiration or a friend.
Thank you Angela Thomas and Maria Savva for reading my ramblings. I'm so grateful for your friendship.
I also want to thank my readers for taking a chance on my ramblings.

About Helle Gade

Helle Gade lives in Denmark. She is a book blogger, poet, photographer, nocturnal creature, avid reader and chocolate addict. She has been writing poetry since 2011 and published four poetry collections since then. She has been fortunate to work with a bunch of brilliant authors and photographers on The Mind's Eye series. Her book Nocturnal Embers won the Best Poetry Collection with eFestival of Words.

Other BDP books by Helle Gade

Terrifying Love - A Halloween Anthology
Beautiful Tragedy - A Halloween Anthology
How To Tame A Wild Tempest
Poesi - A Collection of Poems Volume One
The Fighter
Dolce Amore
Urban Rose
Golden Tattoo - A Halloween Anthology

www.ingramcontent.com/pod-product-compliance
Lightning Source LLC
Chambersburg PA
CBHW010754150726
48196CB00007B/558